D0132119

Homes around the World

Homes on the Move

Nicola Barber

Crabtree Publishing Company

www.crabtreebooks.com

Crabtree Publishing Company

www.crabtreebooks.com

Editors: Hayley Leach, Ellen Rodger, Michael Hodge
Senior Design Manager: Rosamund Saunders
Designer: Elaine Wilkinson
Geography consultant: Ruth Jenkins

Photo credits: Bryan and Cherry Alexander Photography/Alamy p. 25; Pat Behnke/Alamy p. 10; Bill Brooks/Alamy p. 11; Richard Cooke/Alamy p. 23; Neil Cooper/Alamy p. 9; Martin J. Dignard/Alamy p. 13, p. 26; Images of Africa Photobank/Alamy p. 24; Justin Kase/Alamy p. 15; Andrew Waston/Alamy p. 12; Theo Allofs/zefa/Corbis p. 16; Roger Ball/Corbis p. 19; Desmond Boylan/Reuters/Corbis p. 20; Dean Conger/Corbis cover and p. 18; Dave G. Houser/Post Houserstock/Corbis p. 7; Ludovic Maisant/Corbis p. 14; Stephanie Maze/Corbis p. 22; Wendy Stone/Corbis p. 17; Tomasz Tomaszewski/National Geographic/Getty p. 21; Panoramic Images/Getty title page and p. 8; Lonely Planet Images p. 6, p. 27.

Cover: Three yurts in the snow near Lake Tsagaan Nuur in Mongolia.

Title page: This tent is in Tunisia in Africa. It belongs to a group of nomadic people called the Bedouin. The tent is made from camel hair.

Activity & illustrations: Shakespeare Squared pp. 28, 29.

Library and Archives Canada Cataloguing in Publication

Barber, Nicola
    Homes on the move / Nicola Barber.

(Homes around the world)
Includes index.
ISBN 978-0-7787-3544-1 (bound).--ISBN 978-0-7787-3556-4 (pbk.)

1. Dwellings--Juvenile literature. 2. Mobile homes--Juvenile literature.
I. Title. II. Series: Barber, Nicola. Homes around the world.

TX1106.B37 2007   j392.3'6   C2007-904710-6

Library of Congress Cataloging-in-Publication Data

Barber, Nicola.
    Homes on the move / Nicola Barber.
        p. cm. -- (Homes around the world)
    Includes index.
    ISBN-13: 978-0-7787-3544-1 (rlb)
    ISBN-10: 0-7787-3544-3 (rlb)
    ISBN-13: 978-0-7787-3556-4 (pb)
    ISBN-10: 0-7787-3556-7 (pb)
    1. Mobile homes--Juvenile literature. 2. Mobile home living--Juvenile literature. I. Title. II. Series.

TX1106.B37 2008
643'.29--dc22   2007030183

Crabtree Publishing Company

www.crabtreebooks.com   1-800-387-7650

**Published in Canada
Crabtree Publishing**
616 Welland Ave.
St. Catharines, Ontario
L2M 5V6

**Published in the United States
Crabtree Publishing**
PMB 59051
350 Fifth Avenue
59th Floor
New York, NY 10118

Printed in the U.S.A./102011/CG20110916

Published by CRABTREE PUBLISHING COMPANY
Copyright © **2008**

Contents

Words in **bold** can be found in the glossary on page 30

What is a moveable home?

A moveable home is a home that can be moved from place to place. People need to move for many reasons. Some people move around to look for work. Other people move to new places to find food for their animals to eat.

▼ *This home in Kalacha, Kenya, is made from wooden poles covered with cloths. It is light and easy to move.*

There are many kinds of moveable homes, including tents, houseboats, and **yurts**. Some moveable homes have wheels. These homes are called **trailers**. They are **towed** along behind a car or other **vehicle**.

Mobile home
In Noth America, a "mobile home" means a **prefabricated** home or trailer set up in a mobile-home or trailer park.

▲ *This recreational vehicle, or RV, is traveling through the red rocks of the Valley of Fire State Park, in Nevada.*

Tents and shelters

Tents are easy and quick to put up and take down. People who live permanently in tents are usually **nomadic**. Nomadic people move from one place to another, often to find grass for their animals to eat. Every time they move, they take their tents and all their **belongings** with them.

▼ *This tent is in Tunisia in Africa. It belongs to a group of nomadic people called the "Bedouin". The tent is made from camel hair.*

A war or a disaster, such as an **earthquake**, can force people to leave their homes suddenly. People who are forced to leave their homes and live somewhere else are called **refugees**. They often live in **shelters** that can be easily moved.

▲ These refugee families from Somalia, a country in northeast Africa, have built their own shelters in a refugee camp in Ethiopia, Africa.

Trailers and houseboats

The **Roma** and **Travelers** are traditionally nomadic people who live in Europe. In the past, they lived in brightly painted, wooden wagons pulled by horses. Today, many Roma live in permanent homes or trailers.

▼ *Every year many Travelers meet at this horse fair held in Appleby, England.*

Moveable homes on the water are called "houseboats". Some houseboats have their own motors to move around with. Others have to be towed by other boats.

Mobile life

Traditional Roma wagons, or caravans, are called "vardos".

▲ *This houseboat in Burleigh Falls, Ontario, Canada, has its own motor.*

Building a moveable home

The Tuareg people live in the huge Sahara **desert** in northern Africa. To make their homes, they use wooden poles for the **frame**. They then stretch a cover made from goat skins across the poles.

▼ *The Tuareg use **woven** mats to make the sides of their shelters.*

12

In the Arctic, the Inuit people make shelters out of blocks of snow. These snowhouses are called **"igloos"**. Some Inuit build igloos for shelter when they go on hunting trips in the winter. The thick snow blocks keep heat in better than a tent would during the Arctic winter.

▲ *These Inuit people in northern Quebec, Canada, are cutting blocks out of the deep snow to build an igloo.*

13

Inside a moveable home

Across Central Asia, many people live in mobile homes called "yurts". A yurt is built in the shape of a circle. The wall is a criss-cross frame made out of wood from willow trees and covered in thick **felt** mats. The floor is covered in rugs for warmth.

▼ *This yurt is in Uzbekistan. People sit on the carpeted floor to eat their meals.*

In some moveable homes, everything has to be squeezed into a small space. In recreational vehicles, people can sit on long seats during the day. At night, the seats pull across to make a bed.

Mobile life
It is bad luck for anyone to step on the door frame of a yurt when they go in or out of it.

▲ *This camper van has a lot of cupboards above the windows to store things in.*

The weather

Tents are useful moveable homes in hot, dry places, such as deserts. People can put up a tent in the **shade** of a tree to keep it cool. They can open the side of the tent to let cool air in or they can shut the tent to keep strong winds out.

▼ *The tent on this van is used for camping in Australia. Air flows around the tent to keep it cool.*

Mobile homes are sometimes used in wet, rainy places. The Mbuti people live in the **rainforests** of central Africa. They make their homes out of wooden frames covered with large leaves.

▲ The large leaves covering these homes in Ituri forest in the Democratic Republic of Congo help keep the rain out.

The environment

When summer ends, some nomadic people move to warmer places. In Mongolia, many nomadic people spend the summer in the mountains. Their cows, sheep, and goats eat the grass in the high **pastures**. Then the people pack up their homes and move to lower pastures for the cold winter months.

▼ *In Mongolia, nomadic people move their yurts with the* **seasons**. *These yurts stand in the snow near Lake Tsagaan Nuur.*

18

Hurricanes and strong winds can do a lot of damage to mobile homes and trailers. These homes are usually made from light materials, such as metal and plastic, so that people can move them easily. They are not as strong as permanent houses made from stone or brick are.

▲ *Mobile homes and trailers in this trailer park were completely destroyed by a hurricane.*

School and play

Children who live in moveable homes may move around a lot. When they move, they cannot go to the same school all the time. Parents may teach their children at home. Refugee camps sometimes have schools so that children can learn while they are far from home.

▼ *These children go to school in a refugee camp in Nepal, at least 124 miles (200 kilometers) away from where they used to live.*

Moveable homes are often quite small, so children spend a lot of time playing outside. Children from families that move around often play together and become good friends.

▲ *Children play outside a Roma trailer camp in Lourdes, France.*

Going to work

Many people who move from place to place are farmers. When they move, they look for new land to **graze** their animals or a place to grow their crops. When the grass or the soil gets worn out in one place, these farmers look for new land to start again.

▼ This farmer is burning a patch of rainforest in Brazil to clear a space to grow crops.

22

A circus is a group of people who travel around and put on shows in many towns and villages. Circus members include clowns, acrobats, and jugglers, and they live in trailers. The circus happens in a big tent called a "big top".

▲ The big top is surrounded by trailers, where people who work for the circus live.

Getting around

In deserts, people use camels or donkeys to carry their homes from place to place. They fold up their homes and put them on the camels' backs. Camels are very strong, and they can carry heavy loads in hot deserts.

▼ These camels are carrying the frames and mats of Gabbra houses in Maikona, Kenya.

In the Arctic, the Inuit used to travel across the ice and snow on **sleds** pulled by dogs. Today, most Inuit use sleds with motors called **"snowmobiles"**.

Mobile life
Camels have very wide feet, so they can walk on the soft desert sand without sinking.

▲ *These Inuit people are driving their snowmobiles across the ice in Igloolik, Nunavut, Canada. The ice melts in summer.*

25

Where in the world?

Some of the places talked about in this book have been labeled here.

Look at these two pictures carefully.

- How are the homes different from each other?

- What is each home made of?

- Look at their walls and roofs.

- How are these homes different from where you live?

- How are they the same?

NORTH AMERICA

Igloolik

Burleigh Falls

Valley of Fire State Park

ATLANTIC OCEAN

PACIFIC OCEAN

SOUTH AMERICA

Northern Quebec, Canada

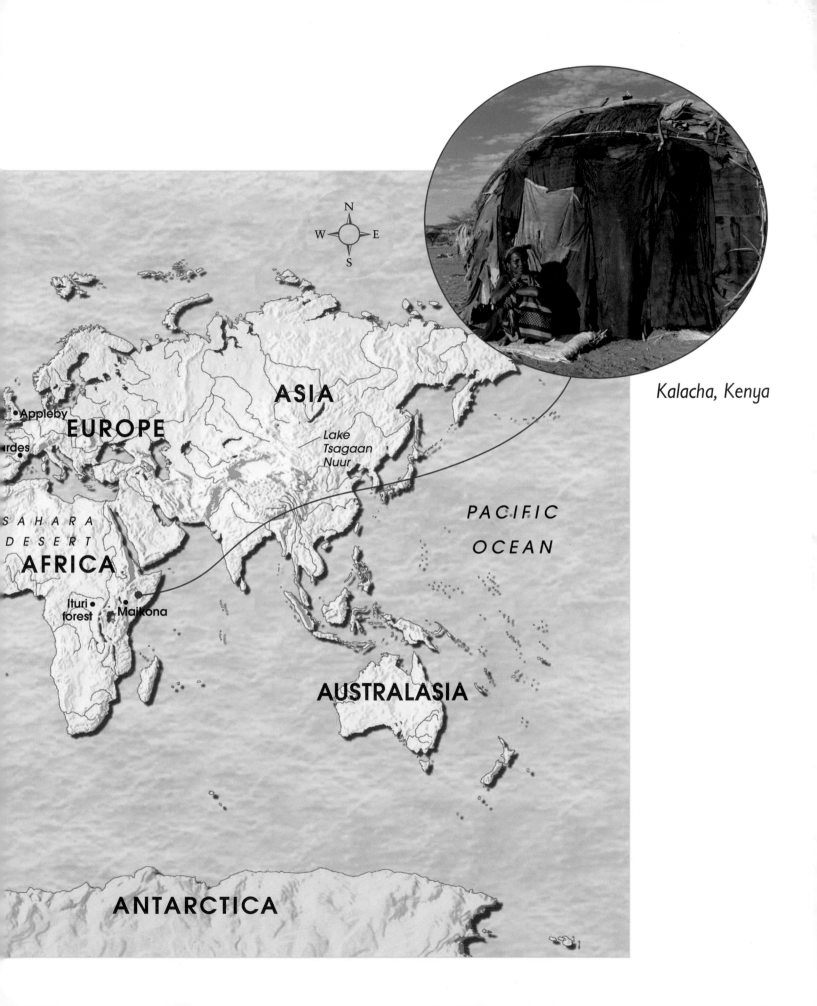

Kalacha, Kenya

EUROPE

ASIA

AFRICA

Appleby

rdes

SAHARA
DESERT

Ituri
forest

Maikona

Lake
Tsagaan
Nuur

PACIFIC

OCEAN

AUSTRALASIA

ANTARCTICA

N

W   E

S

My own igloo

The following activity allows you to make your own igloo out of clay and create a wintry scene.

What you need
- construction paper
- plain white paper
- modeling clay
- rolling pin
- toothpick
- cotton balls
- glue

1. Crumple a piece of plain white paper into a ball. Glue the ball to the middle of a piece of construction paper.
2. Using the rolling pin, roll out your piece of modeling clay so that it makes a flat, square shape. It does not have to be a perfect square. Lay the clay on top of the crumpled paper ball.

3. Press the edges of the clay into the construction paper. You want to make sure that your igloo will not slide or shift. Shape another small piece of clay into an upside down "U." This will be the door to your igloo. Lightly press the door into the igloo. Use the toothpick to draw snow blocks on the igloo.

4. Lightly pull apart a cotton ball. Glue the cotton ball to the construction paper to make snow. Repeat this step several times so that the area around your igloo is covered with the cotton. If you like, you could make small hills out of the cotton to look like mounds of snow.

Now you have your very own igloo. Make sure to display your igloo on a flat surface. Think about what it would be like to live in an igloo. Would you like to live in one for a short time? Why or why not?

Glossary

belongings	The things that people own
desert	A dry area with very little or no rainfall
earthquake	When the ground moves and shakes
felt	A thick, warm fabric made from wool or animal hair
frame	A structure that gives something shape and strength
graze	To eat grass
hurricane	A strong storm with high winds and lots of rain
igloo	A snowhouse
nomads	People who move from place to place, rather than living in one place all the time
pasture	Land covered with grass where animals go to graze
prefabricated	Ready-made or manufactured
rainforest	An area of thick forest with high rainfall in a tropical region
refugees	People who are forced to leave their homes and live somewhere else
Roma	Nomadic and semi-nomadic people of Europe
seasons	Four different times of year with different kinds of weather. The seasons are winter, spring, summer, and autumn.
shade	An area where there is no sun
shelter	Any structure that provides some cover from the weather
sled	A vehicle with runners for moving across snow
snowmobile	A sled with a motor
tow	To pull something behind you
trailer	A mobile home that sometimes has wheels
vehicle	Any kind of transport with wheels, such as a car or a truck
woven	When something has been threaded in and out
yurt	A kind of mobile home used in Central Asia

Further information

Books to read

Homes, from the Discovering World Cultures series

People and Places, from the Secrets of the Rainforest series

Life in the Far North, from the Native Nations of North America series

Life in an Anishinabe Camp, from the Native Nations of North America series

Websites

http://www.ucc.uconn.edu/~epsadm03/mbuti.html

For information about the Mbuti of the Democratic Republic of Congo

http://kids.mongabay.com/elementary/001.html

For information about rainforests

http://collections.ic.gc.ca/arctic/inuit/people.htm

For information about the Inuit

http://www.mongolyurt.com/

For information about yurts

Index

All of the numbers in **bold** refer to photographs.